Dance in Your Pants!

Written by April J. Vidal

© 2025 by April J. Vidal
All rights are happily reserved!

That means no part of this book—not the dancing,
the dreaming, or the delightful rhyming—
can be copied, shared, or used without a cheerful
"okay" from the author.

This is a made-up story celebrating real magic—
the kind that lives in every kid who dares
to dance their own way.

First edition, 2025

ISBN: 978-1-969705-04-5

For every child who dances in their own way, including my own children and my grandchildren…

You are magical just as you are.

In addition, to my brother David Gary who danced by feeling vibration under his feet, who was part of the Deaf Community.

1965–2005

Wiggle your fingers,
wiggle your toes,
Dance in your pants
wherever life goes!
No need for music,
just follow your beat,
With joy in your heart
and light in your feet.

If silence surrouds you, dan't feel alone,
Your dance speaks louder than a ring or a tone.
Feel the vibrations, move with the light,
Dance in your pants with all of your might!

If you use wheels
instead of your shoes,

Spin in your chair
to the rhythm you choose!

You're strong, you're cool,
you're full of grace,

Dance in your pants
all over the place!

If you wear glasses to help you see,
You're still a star, as bright as can be!
Look at the world through your dancing lens,
Dance in your pants with all of your friends!

If colors are hidden
or shapes disappear,
You can still feel the
magic whenever it's near.

With touch and sound
and dreams so wide,
Dance in your pants
from side to side.

Boys who love dancing, boys who leap,
Boys who twirl or glide or sweep —
It's not just for girls, come join the prance
Boys can shine with dance in their pants

If words feel tricky or feelings feel big,
You can twirl, you can jump, you can bounce like a jig!
Autism brings a beautiful view,
Dance in your pants in a way that's true to you.

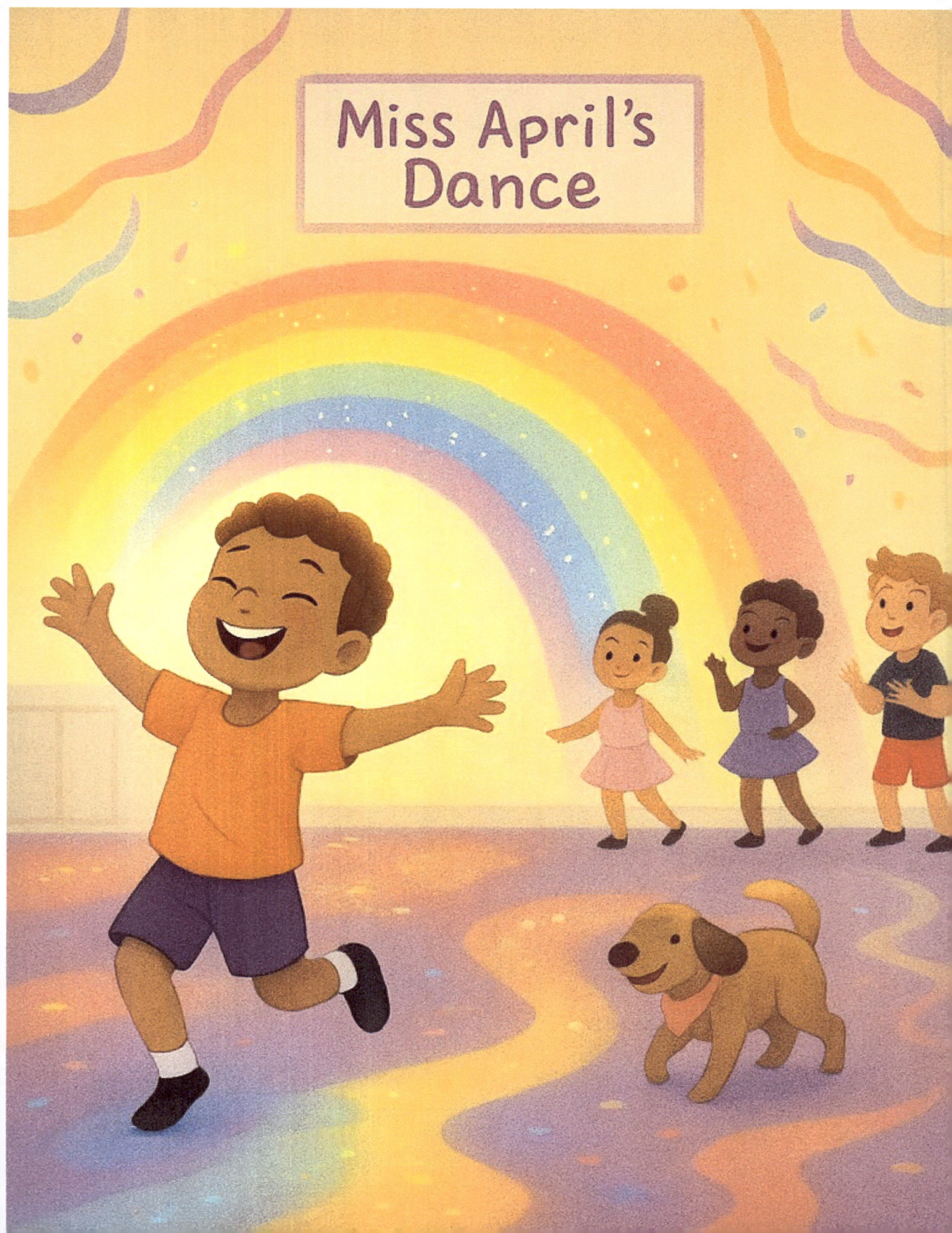

Boys in ballet with shoes so neat,
Flying high with graceful feet —
Strong and proud in every stance,
Dance in your pants, take a chance!

If learning is slower or different or new,
That just means there's more of you to view.
You shine like a star in your own brilliant stance,
Dance in your pants — give life a chance!

Girls who love hip hop beats,
With jumping shoes and moving feet —
Flip your cap and strike your stance,
Dance in your pants, give joy a glance!

If you are small
and quick on your feet,

Tap to the rhythm
with a zippy beat!

Size doesn't matter
when you've got a chance,

To smile, to shine,
and dance in your pants!

From city streets to country farms,
From busy hands to open arms,
From mountains high to oceans wide —
Dance in your pants with joyful pride!

With skin that's dark or light or gold,
Or any shade this world can hold,
You bring color to this global dance,
Dance in your pants — give peace a chance!